Pebble®
Bilingüe/
Bilingual Plus

RAMAS MILITARES/MILITARY BRANCHES

EL EJÉRCITO DE EE.UU. /
THE U.S. ARMY

por/by Matt Doeden

Editor Consultor/Consulting Editor: Dra. Gail Saunders-Smith

Consultor/Consultant: John Grady
Director of Communications, Association of the United States Army

CAPSTONE PRESS
a capstone imprint

Pebble Plus is published by Capstone Press,
151 Good Counsel Drive, P.O. Box 669, Mankato, Minnesota 56002.
www.capstonepress.com

092009
005618CGS10

 Books published by Capstone Press are manufactured with paper
containing at least 10 percent post-consumer waste.

Library of Congress Cataloging-in-Publication Data
Doeden, Matt.
    [U.S. Army. Spanish & English]
    El Ejército de EE.UU. / por Matt Doeden = The U.S. Army / by Matt Doeden.
    p. cm. — (Pebble Plus bilingüe/bilingual. Ramas militares = Military branches)
    Includes index.
    Summary: "Simple text and photographs describe the U.S. Army's purpose, jobs, tools, and
machines — in both English and Spanish" — Provided by publisher.
    ISBN 978-1-4296-4602-4 (library binding)
    1. United States. Army — Juvenile literature. I. Title. II. Title: U.S. Army. III. Series.
UA25.D6418 2010
355.00973 — dc22   2009030382

Editorial Credits
Gillia Olson, editor; Strictly Spanish, translation services; Katy Kudela, bilingual editor; Renée T. Doyle,
    designer; Jo Miller, photo researcher; Eric Manske, production specialist

Photo Credits
DVIC/PH3 Shawn Hussong, 17; SGT Brandon Aird, 7; Sgt 1st Class Robert C. Brogan, 21; SGT Igor Paustovski,
    19; SPC Joshua Balog, 13; SRA Priscilla Robinson, 9; SSGT Eric T. Sheler, 5; SSGT Shane A. Cuomo, 15
Getty Images Inc./AFP/Mauricio Lima, 11
Shutterstock/EchoArt, 3
U.S. Army photo, 1
U.S. Army photo by Staff Sgt Russell L. Klika, front and back cover, 22

Artistic Effects
iStockphoto/Piotr Przeszlo (metal), cover, 1
Shutterstock/Tamer Yazici (camouflage), cover, 1, 24

Note to Parents and Teachers

The Ramas militares/Military Branches set supports national science standards related
to science, technology, and society. This book describes and illustrates the U.S. Army in
both English and Spanish. The images support early readers in understanding the text.
The repetition of words and phrases helps early readers learn new words. This book also
introduces early readers to subject-specific vocabulary words, which are defined in the
Glossary section. Early readers may need assistance to read some words and to use the
Table of Contents, Glossary, Internet Sites, and Index sections of the book.

Table of Contents

Tabla de contenidos

What Is the Army?

The Army is a branch of the United States Armed Forces. People in the Army keep the country safe.

¿Qué es el Ejército?

El Ejército es una rama de las Fuerzas Armadas de Estados Unidos. Las personas que están en el Ejército mantienen la seguridad del país.

Army Jobs

People in the Army are called soldiers. Infantry soldiers fight battles on the ground.

Trabajos en el Ejército

Las personas del Ejército se llaman soldados. Los soldados de infantería combaten batallas en tierra.

Army pilots fly helicopters. Pilots use Black Hawk helicopters to carry soldiers and supplies.

Los pilotos del Ejército vuelan helicópteros. Los pilotos usan helicópteros Black Hawk para transportar soldados y suministros.

Army mechanics fix machines.

Los mecánicos del Ejército

reparan máquinas.

11

The Army has many other jobs. Some soldiers are doctors, cooks, or police officers.

El Ejército tiene muchos más trabajos. Algunos soldados son médicos, cocineros u oficiales de policía.

Tools and Machines

The Army uses tanks.

The M1 Abrams is

its main tank.

Herramientas y máquinas

El Ejército usa tanques.

El M1 Abrams es el

tanque principal.

Soldiers ride in Humvees.
These trucks have armor
to keep soldiers safe.

Los soldados viajan en
Humvees. Estos camiones tienen
una armadura que mantiene
seguros a los soldados.

The Army uses weapons. Soldiers carry M-16 rifles. Grenades and missiles blow up enemy targets.

El Ejército usa armas. Los soldados llevan rifles M-16. Las granadas y misiles hacen explotar los objetivos enemigos.

Keeping Us Safe

The brave soldiers of the Army fight for our country. They risk their lives to keep us safe.

Mantener nuestra seguridad

Los valientes soldados del Ejército combaten por nuestro país. Ellos arriesgan sus vidas para mantener nuestra seguridad.

Glossary

Armed Forces — the whole military; the U.S. Armed Forces include the Army, Navy, Air Force, Marine Corps, and Coast Guard.

armor — a strong covering used to keep things or people safe

branch — a part of a larger group

grenade — a small weapon used to blow up a target

mechanic — a soldier who fixes Army planes, tanks, trucks, and other machines

missile — a large weapon used to blow up a target

rifle — a weapon that can fire bullets very fast

tank — an armored vehicle that moves on two tracks

target — an object at which to aim or shoot

Internet Sites

FactHound offers a safe, fun way to find Internet sites related to this book. All of the sites on FactHound have been researched by our staff.

Here's all you do:

Visit *www.facthound.com*

FactHound will fetch the best sites for you!

Glosario

la armadura — una cobertura fuerte que se usa para mantener la seguridad de las cosas o las personas

las Fuerzas Armadas — todas las ramas militares; las Fuerzas Armadas de EE.UU. incluyen el Ejército, la Armada, la Fuerza Aérea, la Infantería de Marina y la Guardia Costera.

la granada — un arma pequeña que se usa para hacer explotar un objetivo

el mecánico — un soldado que repara los aviones, tanques, camiones y otras máquinas del Ejército

el misil — un arma grande que se usa para hacer explotar un objetivo

el objetivo — un objeto al cual se apunta o se dispara

la rama — una parte de un grupo más grande

el rifle — un arma que puede disparar balas rápidamente

el tanque — un vehículo armado que se mueve con dos orugas

Sitios de Internet

FactHound brinda una forma segura y divertida de encontrar sitios de Internet relacionados con este libro. Todos los sitios en FactHound han sido investigados por nuestro personal.

Esto es todo lo que tú necesitas hacer:

Visita *www.facthound.com*

¡FactHound buscará los mejores sitios para ti!

Index

Índice